The All About Series

All About ... Canadian Animals

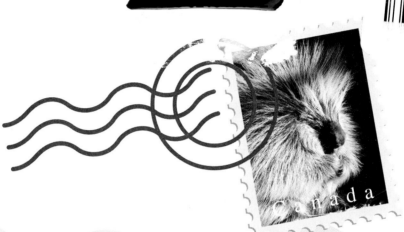

Canada

Porcupines

Barb McDermott and Gail McKeown
Reidmore Books

Reidmore Books Inc.

For more information contact
Nelson Thomson Learning,
1120 Birchmount Road,
Scarborough, Ontario,
M1K 5G4.
Or you can visit our
internet site at
http://www.nelson.com

Printed and bound in Canada
3 4 5   03 02 01

Canadian Cataloguing in Publication Data
McDermott, Barb.
All about Canadian animals : porcupines

(All about series)
Includes index.
ISBN 1-896132-29-4

North American porcupine--Juvenile literature. I. McKeown, Gail. II. Title. III. Series:
McDermott, Barb. All about series.
QL737.R65M32 1998   j599.35'974   C98-910192-4

About the Authors

Barb McDermott and Gail McKeown are highly experienced
kindergarten teachers living in Ontario. Both hold Bachelor of Arts and
Bachelor of Education degrees, Early Childhood diplomas, specialist
certificates in Primary Education, and have completed qualification
courses in Special Education. As well, Gail has a specialist certificate in
Reading and Visual Arts, and Barb has one in Guidance.

Credits

Editorial: Leah-Ann Lymer, Scott Woodley
Illustration, design and layout: Bruno Enderlin, David Strand

Photo Credits
Entries are by page number
Abbreviations: VU=Visuals Unlimited
Cover photo: VU/Bill Banaszewski
Stamp photo: Sarah Gjosund
Page
1 VU/Joe McDonald
3 VU/Joe McDonald
5 VU/Gerald and Buff Corsi
7 The Russ Heinl Group/Image Network Inc.
9 Barbara Gerlach
11 VU/John D. Cunningham
13 VU/D. Cavagnaro
15 VU/Gerald and Buff Corsi
17 VU/Joe McDonald
19 Sarah Gjosund
21 VU/Doug Sokell
23 VU/Joe McDonald
25 VU/Ron Spomer
27 VU/Tom J. Ulrich

We have made every effort to identify and credit the sources of
all photographs, illustrations, and information used in this
book. Reidmore Books appreciates any further information or
corrections; acknowledgment will be given in subsequent editions.

Table of Contents

(All about what's in the book)

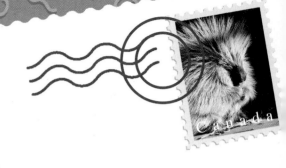

Appearance
(All about what porcupines look like)

Porcupines are **mammals** of the forests.

Porcupines belong to the rodent family.

Porcupines can live 10 years.

Porcupines have a short, **blunt nosed** face.

Porcupines have small eyes and round ears.

Porcupines can weigh 18 kg.

Porcupines have short, **bowed legs**.

A Porcupine

Appearance
(All about what porcupines look like)

Porcupines can be 1 m long.

Porcupines have **humped shoulders**.

Porcupines have a soft, brown, woolly undercoat.

Porcupines have a coarse, long, brown overcoat.

Porcupines have a coat of **quills** that come out when they are scared.

Porcupines have no quills on their face, legs, or stomach.

A Porcupine with Quills Up

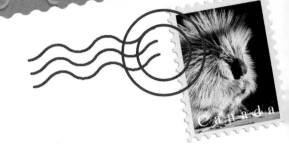

Habitat
(All about where porcupines live)

Porcupines live in **thickets** along rivers.

Porcupines spend a lot of time in trees.

Porcupines live alone.

Porcupines sometimes share a **den**.

Porcupines

Habitat
(All about where porcupines live)

There are **dangers** in the habitat of porcupines because they are slow moving animals.

Porcupines often die in forest fires.

Porcupines are also killed on roads by cars.

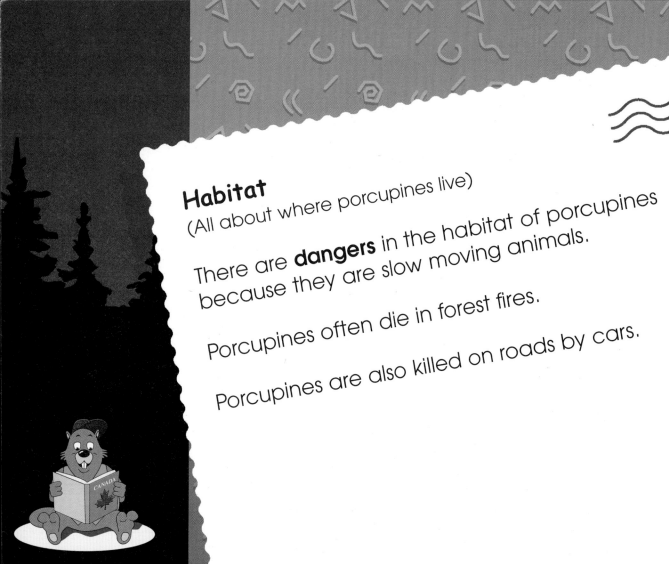

A Forest Fire

7

Diet
(All about what porcupines eat)

Porcupines are **herbivores**.

Porcupines eat tree bark, leaves, twigs, and plants.

Porcupines eat flowers, weeds, acorns, grass, and clover.

Porcupines will chew bones and old antlers.

Porcupines Eat Bark

Diet
(All about what porcupines eat)

Porcupines chew noisily.

Porcupines eat very slowly.

Porcupines have 12 grinding teeth in the back of their mouth.

Porcupines have orange coloured teeth that never stop growing.

Porcupines are **nocturnal** most of the year.

Orange Porcupine Teeth

Predators
(All about the enemies of porcupines)

The enemies of porcupines are dogs, red foxes, wolves, coyotes, cougars, lynxes, and bears.

Porcupines will hide from their enemies.

Porcupines will **hunch** their backs and show their quills when frightened.

Porcupines will hit their enemies with their tail.

When an animal touches a quill, the quill will stick into the animal's skin.

The quill hurts the animal.

A Dog with Quills in Its Mouth

Offspring
(All about porcupine babies)

Porcupine babies are born in a rock pile or a log stump.

Porcupine babies drink milk from their mother.

Porcupine babies are well developed at birth.

Porcupine babies are born with teeth.

A Porcupine Baby

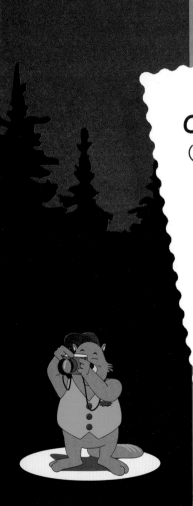

Offspring
(All about porcupine babies)

Porcupines have 1 baby in the spring.

Porcupine babies are born with soft quills.

The quills are **hidden** with hair.

Porcupine babies can climb 2 days after they are born.

Baby Quills Are Soft

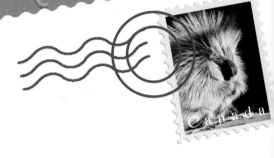

Adaptation
(All about how porcupines live in their world)

Porcupines have a good sense of smell.

Porcupines have a thick, **muscular** tail.

Porcupines use their tail as a weapon.

Porcupines have long, curved **claws**.

Porcupines use their claws for digging and feeding.

Porcupine Tail

Adaptation
(All about how porcupines live in their world)

Porcupines are good at climbing trees.

Their back feet help them to climb.

Porcupines are **flat footed**.

Porcupines like to stay in their home when it rains and snows.

Porcupines move about when it is dry.

Porcupines Climb Trees

Special Characteristics
(All about what makes porcupines interesting)

Porcupines can have 30 000 quills.

The quills can be 8 cm long.

Porcupine quills are filled with air.

Porcupine quills help porcupines to float in water.

Porcupine Quills

23

Special Characteristics
(All about what makes porcupines interesting)

Porcupines move very slowly.

Porcupines stay close to their homes most of the year.

Porcupines like to chew.

Porcupines have strong teeth.

Porcupines have upper and lower **incisor** teeth for biting.

A Porcupine in Its Den

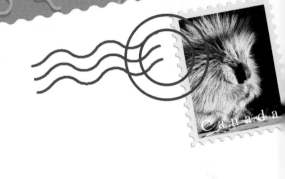

Summary
(All about the ending)

Porcupines move slowly.

Porcupines use their quills to protect themselves.

Porcupines eat bark and plants.

Porcupines are truly amazing animals ... that live in Canada.

A Porcupine in Winter

Glossary
(All about what the words mean)

blunt nosed (page 1)
Blunt nosed refers to a rounded nose rather than a pointy nose.

bowed legs (page 1)
Bowed legs are curved outward.

claws (page 18)
Claws are sharp nails on the feet of animals.

dangers (page 6)
Dangers are things that may cause harm.

den (page 4)
A den is a place where a wild animal lives.

flat footed (page 20)
Flat footed refers to walking on the whole bottom of the foot.

herbivores (page 8)
Herbivores are animals who eat plants.

hidden (page 16)
Hidden means cannot be seen.

humped shoulders (page 2)
Humped shoulders refer to rounded shoulders.

hunch (page 12)
To hunch is to bend over or form into a hump.

incisor (page 24)
An incisor is a sharp tooth used for cutting and tearing.

mammals (page 1)
Mammals are animals who feed their babies milk.

muscular (page 18)
Muscular means strong.

nocturnal (page 10)
Nocturnal means active during the night instead of the day.

quills (page 2)
Quills are stiff, sharp spines on a porcupine.

thickets (page 4)
Thickets are groups of bushes or small trees.